I0902666

IMAGES
of America

LAKE CITY AND COLUMBIA COUNTY

The building with the most noteworthy architecture in downtown Lake City is the Columbia County Courthouse, built in 1902. There have been a few courthouses throughout the county's history, but the present-day courthouse has stood by Lake DeSoto for 118 years. This photograph shows it in 1948. The dome has since been removed and replaced. (State Archives of Florida.)

On the Cover: This c. 1910 photograph shows men and boys in front of Porter and Glover Dry Goods in downtown Lake City. A Mr. Porter and his brother-in-law Thomas Glover operated the store. (State Archives of Florida.)

IMAGES
of America

LAKE CITY AND COLUMBIA COUNTY

Andrew R. Nicholas

ARCADIA
PUBLISHING

ISBN 978-1-4671-0500-2

Published by Arcadia Publishing
Charleston, South Carolina

Printed in the United States of America

Library of Congress Control Number: 2020932857

For all general information, please contact Arcadia Publishing:
Telephone 843-853-2070
Fax 843-853-0044
E-mail sales@arcadiapublishing.com
For customer service and orders:
Toll-Free 1-888-313-2665

Visit us on the Internet at www.arcadiapublishing.com

This book is dedicated to my wife, Sarah; my mother, Lisa; and the Lake City–Columbia County Historical Museum.

Contents

ACKNOWLEDGMENTS

I want to thank my mother, Lisa Moody, for assisting me in acquiring many of the photographs used in this publication. I could not have completed this book without her help. A Lake City local, Dr. Christopher M. Esing, was a tremendous help in compiling the photographs and information. Dr. Esing is one of the most important historians of Lake City and has gone to great lengths to record and preserve its history. Dr. Sean McMahon, a professor of history at Florida Gateway College, was another historian who helped me at the Lake City–Columbia County Historical Museum. I want to also thank the museum for providing me with photographs, information, and guidance in gathering the material.

H. Morris Williams is another citizen of Lake City who has gone to extraordinary lengths preserving historical photographs and documents. Williams has preserved many photographs in relation to Columbia County education and has essentially established a museum at the Columbia County School Board building to display his work. His son Chris has continued preserving the history of Columbia County education by going through each piece of his father's work and digitizing it on his website, www.lakecityhistory.com. Laura Norris and her generosity in sharing the photographs and stories of First Methodist Church and her father, Bascom Norris, helped me better understand the local fair in Lake City, as well as his philosophy that we must always go the distance in helping those in need.

Throughout the course of working on this publication, I referred to *A History of Columbia County* by Edward Keuchel, *Lake City Florida: A Sesquicentennial Tribute* by Morris Williams and Kevin McCarthy, various documents from the State Archives of Florida, and of course, the local residents themselves on relevant information. For more details on Lake City and Columbia County, I would recommend Keuchel's *A History of Columbia County*, as he went into great detail on many aspects of the topic.

INTRODUCTION

Growing up in nearby Jacksonville, Florida, I would occasionally drive over to Lake City to get away from the hustle and bustle of the big city. The small Southern town had a charming atmosphere that the big city of Jacksonville lacked. I enjoyed walks around the downtown park and Lake DeSoto, as it was quiet with pleasant people also absorbing the charm of the town. Venturing beyond Lake City leads to the countryside of Columbia County, consisting of numerous farms. It was beyond Lake City that I would visit the Ichetucknee River, near the small town of Fort White and O'Leno State Park, to enjoy a relaxing cruise downstream looking through the blue water into a world of underwater beauty. After absorbing the Columbia County environment and the beauty of O'Leno State Park, I would return to Lake City.

Lake City shares its name with many other US towns and cities. Like North Central Florida, Lake City has a rich past. Lake City and Columbia County can trace their history to the days of Spanish Florida, when Hernando de Soto visited the area in 1539. By the early 1800s, the area of present-day Lake City was settled by the Seminole with the establishment of Alligator. The town was named after Halpatter Tustenuggee, or "Alligator Warrior." By the time Americans began to settle here in the early 1820s, the Seminoles abandoned Alligator. In 1832, Columbia County was created, and Newnansville was made the county seat until 1839, when it was moved to Alligator. The name Columbia comes from Christopher Columbus, and is a poetic name for the United States. In 1859, Alligator was incorporated and renamed Lake City. There are several lakes in the vicinity of downtown, including one named Alligator Lake.

Lake City has grown to become one of the largest towns in North Central Florida. Its strategic location during the Civil War led to its attempted capture by the Union army on its march toward Tallahassee in 1863. The Union army was stopped 10 miles east of Lake City, near a creek called Olustee, by Confederate troops that had marched out to meet the Union threat. After the war, Lake City made great progress in education. The University of Florida can trace its history to Lake City in the 1880s, when the Florida Agricultural College was here. The college was renamed the University of Florida in 1905, but unfortunately, it moved to Gainesville. Coincidently, the school's mascot is the gator.

Lake City established Columbia College to replace the University of Florida, but it lasted only 10 years. The old University of Florida campus at Lake City was converted into the present-day Veterans Administration (VA) hospital. Over time, the old university buildings were all demolished and replaced by more modern buildings to meet the needs of the VA. Not far from the VA hospital is the Lake City Gateway Airport, which was Naval Air Station Lake City during World War II. After the war, the airport was named Lake City Municipal Airport and in 2011 was renamed Lake City Gateway Airport. It currently is used by private aircraft. Next to the airport is Florida Gateway College, which was established in 1947 and has become a permanent college for Lake City, returning the town as an education center for this part of Florida.

Lake City is 160 years old, but including its time as Alligator, the town is actually around 200 years old as of 2020. The exact date when Alligator was established is not known, but evidence indicates that it was in the early 1820s. Over 150 years later, the Civil War Battle of Olustee is still commemorated in Lake City to honor the Union and Confederate soldiers. Minus a few that were demolished, the buildings of downtown Lake City on Marion Avenue are over 100 years old, and their exteriors are mostly unchanged to this day.

Lake City's extensive history is seen in the multitude of photographs, postcards, and maps included in this book. The photographs are from the State Archives of Florida, the Lake City–Columbia County Museum, the H. Morris Williams Collection, and local individuals. This publication is intended to preserve the history of the town and to share it with those outside of Columbia County—many of whom may be unaware of one of the most notable towns named Lake City in the United States.

One

Alligator and the 19th Century

Spanish explorer Hernando de Soto was one of the first Europeans to come to the area of present-day Columbia County. De Soto arrived near Tampa Bay in 1539 and marched north with his men. It was in this area that De Soto began to turn west, and it was here that he encountered the Native Americans known as the Timucuans. There are a number of places named after Hernando DeSoto throughout the United States, including Lake DeSoto in downtown Lake City. The Spanish continued to come to the area, and around 1650, a mission was established near the Ichtetucknee River, a six-mile branch of the Santa Fe River. The mission site on the Ichetucknee was destroyed and lost until archaeological expeditions in the 1950s by John Goggin and in the 1980s by Brent Richards Weisman uncovered Timucuan and Spanish artifacts and the remains of the mission. The site is known as Fig Springs. This postcard of Lake De Soto is from around 1890. (Tom and Sue Rowand collection, Dr. Christopher M. Esing.)

There are a number of places named after Hernando De Soto throughout the United States, including Lake DeSoto in downtown Lake City. This photograph of Lake DeSoto from the 1880s shows what appears to be a banana farm, which was most likely destroyed in the Great Freeze of 1894–1895. The photograph was taken from a house on East Duval Street. The development of Alligator and Lake City centered around Lake DeSoto. (Lake City–Columbia County Historical Museum.)

Lake DeSoto can be seen from the roof of the present courthouse in the 1930s. Twentieth-century development, such as a paved road circling the lake, can also be seen around the lake. A courthouse building was later constructed on the part of the park seen here. (State Archives of Florida.)

The site of present-day Lake City was settled in the early 1800s as Alpata Telophka, or "Alligator Town," by Seminole chief Halpatter Tustenuggee, or "Alligator Warrior." Alligator was one of the main leaders of the Dade massacre, which started the Second Seminole War in 1835. To bring awareness to the early history of Lake City and Columbia County, the Alligator Warrior Festival is held at O'Leno State Park. The Battle of San Felasco Hammock, fought in 1836 during the Seminole War, is reenacted annually at the festival. (Author's collection.)

Lake Isabella is about half a mile from Lake DeSoto. Houses from the late 19th to the early 20th centuries surround the lake, making up what is today the Lake Isabella Historic Residential District. According to Lake City natives, the lake was named after Queen Isabella of Spain. (State Archives of Florida.)

Lake Lona is about eight miles west of downtown Lake City. This photograph shows the lake in the early 20th century. Since then, half of the lake has dried up. Lake Lona Elementary School was established in 1928 near the lake. It was in use for 35 years until closing in 1963. (Lake City–Columbia County Historical Museum.)

This aerial photograph of Lake City was taken in 1949. Lake DeSoto is the oval-shaped lake near the center, and Lake Isabella is half a mile south of that. Lake Montgomery, also called Lake Hamburg, is in the center and looks somewhat like a Native American arrowhead. Lake Montgomery is much bigger today. Gwen Lake is at center-left and almost looks like a capital letter D. Harper Lake is on the far left with a smaller lake half a mile south. At bottom right is a portion of Alligator Lake. (University of Florida.)

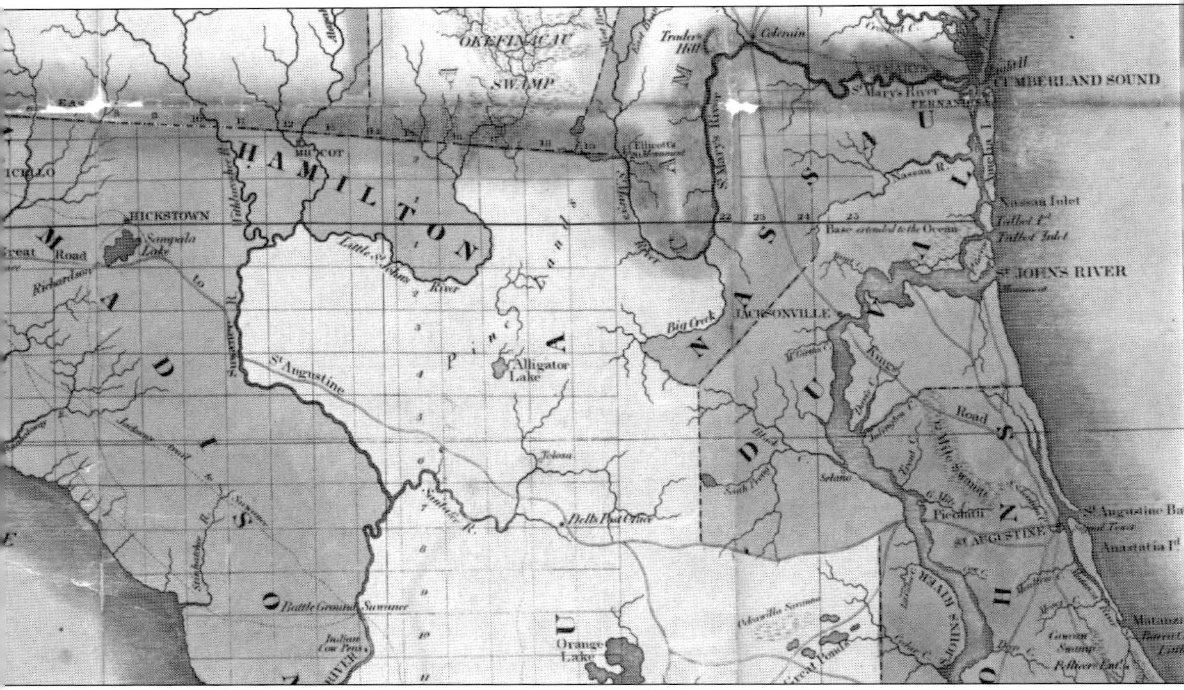

Florida was ceded to the United States by Spain in 1819 as part of the Adams-Onís Treaty. At this time, Florida was split into two regions, West Florida and East Florida. Present-day Lake City was part of East Florida. The Territory of Florida was created in 1822 when East Florida and West Florida were merged. Duval County was also created in 1822, extending all the way to present-day Columbia County. On December 29, 1824, Alachua County was created by the Florida legislature and present-day Columbia County became part of it. This map, produced by Fielding Lucas and I.G. Searcy, shows northern Alachua County in 1829. Alligator, sometimes absent from maps around this time, is north of Alligator Lake. (University of Florida.)

Alligator Lake was named after Chief Halpatter Tustenuggee, or Alligator Warrior. It was near this lake that his Seminole town Alpata Telophka was located. Chief Alligator and the villagers abandoned Alligator and moved to Central Florida in the 1810s. There is no trace of the Seminole town today—only accounts from early settlers who visited the abandoned village in the 1820s. This photograph of Alligator Lake was taken in the 1920s. (State Archives of Florida.)

Tustenuggee United Methodist Church was founded in 1845 by Methodists living near present-day Fort White. The first services were in a log structure once used by workers building the Bellamy Road. The Bellamy Road was named after John Bellamy and connected St. Augustine to Tallahassee, becoming one of Florida's first highways. A portion of the Bellamy Road runs through southern Columbia County near the church. The first pastor of Tustenuggee was Rev. J.C. Ley. In 1868, a frame building was erected but was destroyed by the 1896 Cedar Keys hurricane. The present-day church building was constructed in 1896. (Author's collection.)

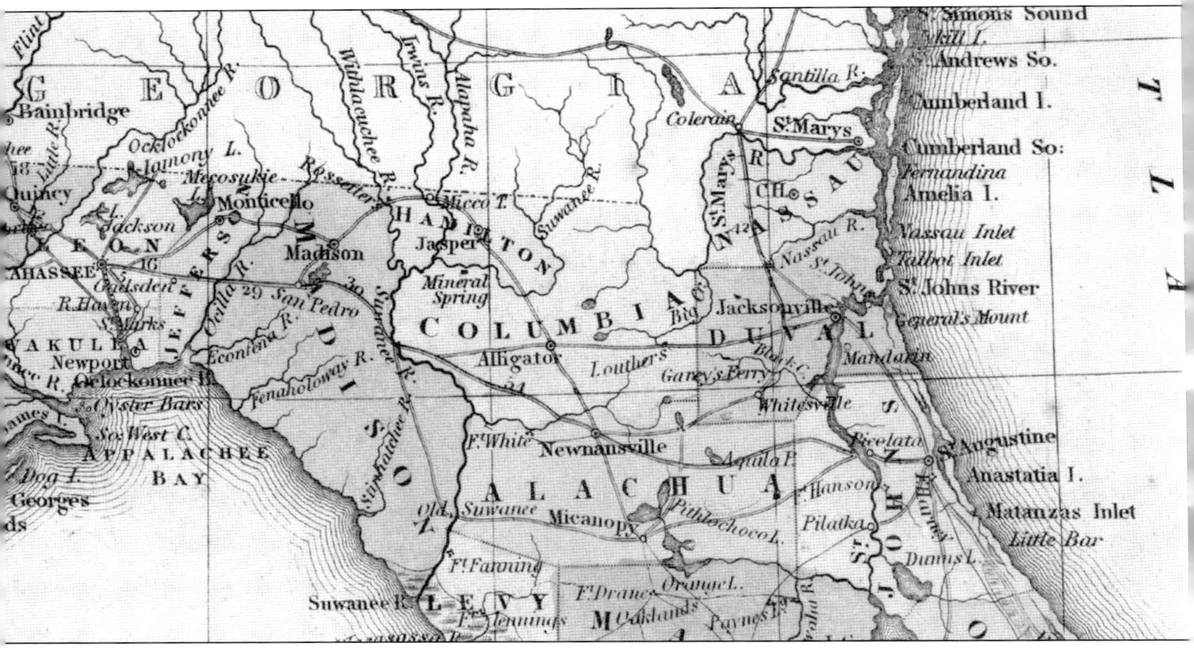

In 1832, Columbia County was created out of Alachua County. Newnansville was the seat of Columbia County until 1839, when Alachua County reabsorbed the town. Alligator became the seat of Columbia County in 1839 and has remained the county seat for 180 years. This portion of Henry Schenck Tanner's map of Florida shows Columbia County in 1849. The county previously comprised the present-day Suwannee, Baker, Bradsford, and Union Counties. (University of Florida.)

Alligator was renamed Fort Lancaster in honor of Judge Joseph Bradford Lancaster, of the Whig Party. The names Fort Lancaster and Alligator were used interchangeably on maps throughout the 1830s, but locals just called the town Lancaster. By 1844, the town reverted to the name Alligator. Fort Lancaster stood at the site of the First National Bank Building, seen in this photograph from 1910. The building is today the city hall of Lake City. A plaque on the front reads, "Site of Fort Lancaster 1835." (State Archives of Florida.)

Joseph Bradford Lancaster was born in 1790 in Kentucky. In 1822, his friend William Pope Duval persuaded him to move to Florida. Duval was the territorial governor of Florida from 1822 to 1834. Lancaster became the mayor of Jacksonville from 1846 to 1847, speaker of the Florida House of Representatives, and a judge on the Florida Supreme Court from 1848 to 1853. He was the first mayor of Tampa in 1856 but died on November 25 of that year after only serving for a few months. (State Archives of Florida.)

The Santa Fe River forms Columbia County's southern border with Alachua and Gilchrist Counties. The name is Spanish for "Holy Faith." Boating on the Santa Fe is a common activity for Columbia County citizens. This photograph shows some boats beached along the Santa Fe River in 1961. (State Archives of Florida.)

The Suwannee River is the northwestern border of Columbia County. Recreational boating is common here too, as seen in this photograph from 1958. The Suwannee became famous from Stephen Foster's song "Old Folks at Home," published in 1851, which is now the state song of Florida. There was once a community on the Suwannee River called Suwannee Shoals that in 1885 had two churches, a school, and 75 families. The first person to settle in Suwannee Shoals was David Gillit, in 1830. (State Archives of Florida.)

The Ichetucknee River is a popular destination for outdoor activities. The most popular is tubing. Many tubing rental companies have been established near the entrance to Ichetucknee Springs State Park. This photograph is from 1970, but similar sights are still seen on the river today. (State Archives of Florida.)

The area that is today O'Leno State Park first began as the town of Keno, on Wire and Bellamy Roads. The earliest known resident of the town was Henry Matier in 1840. The town grew with mills and dams on the nearby Santa Fe River. Keno had a hotel, blacksmith shop, doctor's office, and a general store. It also had a bar and a casino to help relieve boredom. This 1901 photograph shows a picnic outing on the Santa Fe. (State Archives of Florida.)

In 1935, the Florida Forest Service bought the land where the old Keno town was located. The name "old Leno" was used by locals to refer to the former town. This eventually combined to form the name O'Leno, which is still in use today. The Florida Forest Service's goal in acquiring the land was to create a camp for forestry education. The camp was started by the Works Progress Administration near O'Leno. The Civilian Conservation Corps (CCC) created O'Leno State Park in the 1930s as one of Florida's first state parks and as part of Pres. Franklin D. Roosevelt's New Deal program for work relief during the Great Depression. The suspension bridge seen here was created by the CCC in the 1930s. (State Archives of Florida.)

Col. George Michael "Mike" Whetstone operated a general store in the 1870s at Keno. Whetstone named the town after a bingo-type gambling game because he felt that establishing a town in this location was risky. Whetstone applied for a post office for Keno in 1876, but it was denied because the name was associated with gambling. Whetstone changed the name of the town to Leno to make it more appealing. The post office was approved and placed above Whetstone's general store. It was relocated to Mikesville three miles away in 1890. Mikesville is where Whetstone had another residence and is named after him. In 1894, a railroad from Lake City to Fort White was established, bypassing the town of Leno. Because of this and the area being hit hard by the Great Freeze of 1894–1895, the town declined, and its citizens moved to more prosperous areas of Columbia County. The former residents of Leno took most of the lumber and materials from the town with them, leaving only a few foundations. (O'Leno State Park.)

Between 1935 and 1936, the CCC constructed roads, cleared land, and built many of the buildings that still stand today in O'Leno State Park. Camp O'Leno opened in 1938 as part of the Florida Forest Service. For two years, the camp trained youth and other employees in forestry; it transferred to the Florida Park Service in 1940 when it became one of Florida's nine original state parks. This 1936 photograph shows one of the cabins built by the CCC. (State Archives of Florida.)

Noel Raulerson was born around 1790. He served in the 745th Battalion of the Georgia Militia under Capt. William Walker, and with Capt. Richard Walker's Wayne County Mounted Volunteers in the War of 1812. Around 1821, Raulerson, with his wife, Eleanor, and children, moved to Florida, settling on the present-day site of the Columbia County Courthouse. The Raulersons did not stay in Florida for long and returned to Wayne County, Georgia. Noel Raulerson died around 1839. This photograph shows his wife, Eleanor, and son Noel Raulerson Jr. (Lake City–Columbia County Historical Museum.)

Theophilus Weeks was a private in the 6th Regiment of the North Carolina line during the American Revolutionary War. After the war, he returned to his home county of Carteret, North Carolina, where he married Ann O'Steen around 1782. Weeks and his family relocated to Camden County, Georgia, around 1803, then briefly to Louisiana, and finally, Alligator. Weeks remained in Alligator until his death in 1839. He was one of the few Revolutionary War veterans to be buried in Columbia County. The Weeks and O'Steen families are two of the early families that settled in Alligator. This is his grave at Price Creek Cemetery. (Sean McMahon.)

The photograph shows Zachariah Roberts Jr., the son of Mary Weeks and Zachariah Roberts. His mother was the daughter of Theophilus Weeks, and his father served in the War of 1812 and the Seminole Wars. In the early 1820s, the Roberts family moved to Alligator where Zachariah Sr. helped establish the Old Bethel Methodist Church. The family lived in a small cabin on the east side of Alligator Lake. (Lake City–Columbia County Historical Museum.)

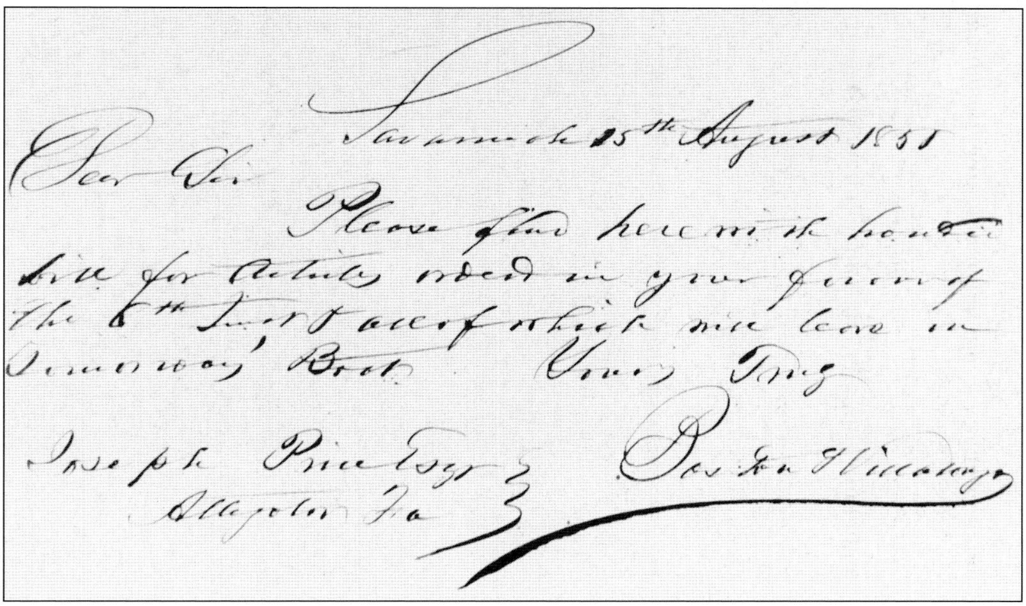

Savannah 25th August 1858

Dear Sir

Please find herewith the [illegible] bill for Articles ordered in your favor of the 6th Inst all of which we leave in [illegible] Boat. Yours Truly

Joseph Price Esqr
Alligator Fla

[illegible]

Alligator did not get a post office until May 22, 1830, but the town did have mail service beginning in 1826. The first post office was discontinued on October 31, 1831, but was reestablished two years later on February 28, 1833. John W. Roberts was the first postmaster, and his house served as both a post office and the courthouse for Columbia County. In the 1830s, mail to and from Alligator usually took about two weeks to deliver. This letter was written in Alligator on August 25, 1858. (State Archives of Florida.)

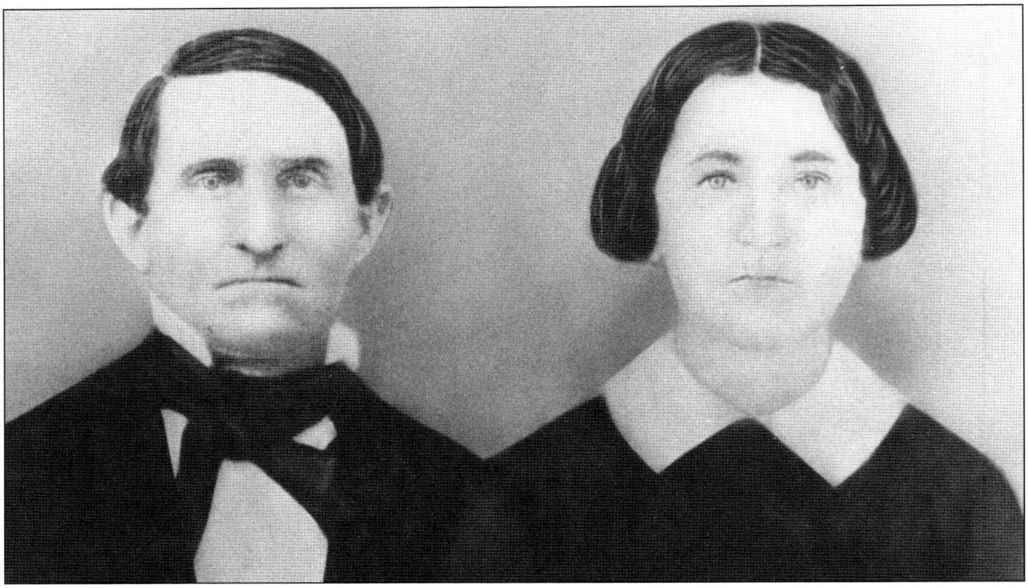

The Goodbread family is one of the earliest in Columbia County. They began with Jacob Tapley Goodbread, born in Camden County, Georgia, on March 28, 1811, to Catherine and Philip Goodbread. Jacob was the brother of Adam Sowder Goodbread, a representative of Florida's 14th District in 1845 and 16th District in 1846. Jacob Goodbread was second lieutenant of a militia company called the Camden County Chasseurs and sheriff of Camden County from 1841 to 1843. When he moved to Columbia County in 1843, he became a county commissioner from 1847 to 1849. He was a wealthy planter and one of the largest slaveholders in the county. This photograph shows Jacob Goodbread and his wife, Jane Dean Brown Goodbread. (State Archives of Florida.)

Corinth Methodist Cemetery was established as a Goodbread cemetery, beginning with the death of Jacob Goodbread's son Hugh Brown Goodbread in 1853 and his wife, Jane, in 1861. Jacob died in 1869 and was also buried here. Since the cemetery's foundation, the Goodbread family and its descendants have been buried there. Corinth Methodist Church was established on the site of the cemetery in 1882. The church was remodeled in 1914 and still stands today. (Author's collection.)

Falling Creek Falls is one of a few waterfalls in Florida. It is about six miles north of Lake City. A church near the falls, Falling Creek Methodist Church, was established in 1865 and is one of the oldest churches in the area. Florida Agricultural College engineering student Edward Orville Powers took this photograph of the falls. (University of Florida.)

William "Billy" Cone was born in North Carolina around 1777 to William and Keziah Cone. The Cone family moved to Camden County, Georgia, where Billy spent most of his youth. He married Sarah Haddock around 1812 and was greatly involved in politics, serving as a representative from Glynn County, justice of the peace, and a representative from Camden County to the Georgia legislature. During the War of 1812, Cone commanded a militia that successfully defended St. Marys, Georgia, against the British. In the Seminole Wars, he was a captain in the Okefenokee Swamp. Cone and his family moved to Columbia County, Florida, by 1840, where he became a member of the territorial legislature. Billy Cone became the patriarch of the Cone family of Columbia County. (State Archives of Florida.)

This photograph shows two of Capt. Billy Cone's sons, James Barnard Cone (left) and William Haddock Cone. Like his father, William also served in the military and engaged in politics. From 1854 to 1856, he represented Columbia County in the Florida Senate. He was captain of his company in the 1st Regiment of Mounted Florida Volunteers in the Third Seminole War in 1857. On August 12, 1863, he enlisted in the Civil War with the 2nd Florida Cavalry, Company G, and became captain of the company. James served under his brother in William's Company of Mounted Volunteers in the Third Seminole War as a lieutenant. He also served as a sergeant in the 2nd Florida Cavalry, Company K. Not pictured is brother Charles Floyd Cone, a captain during the Civil War. (State Archives of Florida.)

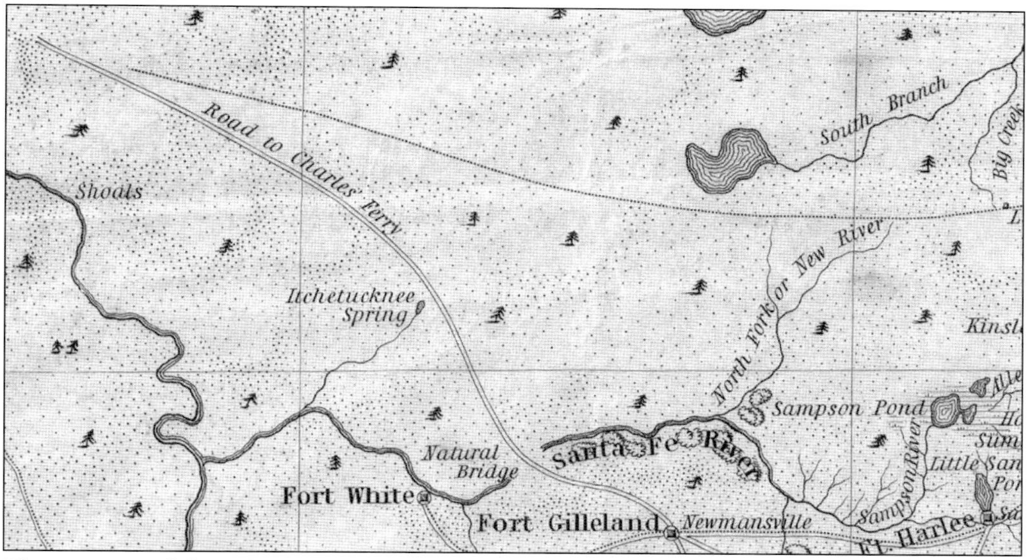

This portion of the US Army Corps of Engineers' 1839 map shows the seat of war in Florida during the Second Seminole War. The original Fort White is seen on the Santa Fe River. It was established in 1837 by a detachment of volunteers during the war. The town of Fort White was founded in 1870 and was briefly the second largest city in Columbia County, with a population of nearly 2,000. It declined following freezes in the winter of 1896–1897 that destroyed the local citrus industry. Phosphate mining ceased by 1910, and cotton farming ended before World War I. The Old Fort White School, built in 1915, is one of the few remaining buildings in the town from this era. (University of Florida.)

This 1937 aerial photograph of southwestern Columbia County shows Fort White at far right. Traveling northwest on US Highway 27, the road going through Fort White leads to the Ichetucknee River and the town of Branford. Traveling southeast on US Highway 47 from Fort White leads to the town of High Springs. (University of Florida.)

The town of Lulu was originally called Hagen. Since Alachua County had a similar-sounding town, Hague , Hagen's mail would often get mixed up with Hague's. Walter Gillen suggested the name of his girlfriend, and Lulu was accepted. Pictured is one of a few stores in Lulu in the 1940s. (Lake City–Columbia County Historical Museum.)

The Cone family home in Benton is seen here around 1900. Standing by the fence are, from left to right, Daniel Cone Jr., his daughter Amy, and son Jack. Daniel's father, Daniel Cone Sr., was a police officer and was killed while on duty on December 6, 1841, in Benton, a small community in northern Columbia County along the Suwannee River. (State Archives of Florida.)

Columbia City is a small community south of Lake City. It features Columbia City Elementary, several churches, a fire station, and Rose Creek. Columbia City was once the location of Gov. George Drew's sawmill, established in 1887. Drew was governor of Florida from 1877 to 1881. (Author's collection.)

The area that was first known as Ellisville was settled by Giles U. Ellis, seen in this sketch, in 1845. Barrsville, in the vicinity of Ellisville, was then settled by James "Jim" Barrs of Brooks County, Georgia. What became known as Barrsville was initially a settlement by Barrs for cultivating citrus fruit on a plat belonging to Giles Ellis. The nearby community of Mount Tabor, named after the Mount Tabor Methodist Episcopal Church, which was constituted in 1854, was also settled for cultivating citrus. In 1871, Barrs opened a general store, which became the location for a post office. In 1872, a shooting occurred at Barr's general store that wounded Jim and mortally wounded his cousin John Barrs. Jim died in 1887, the same year the trial for the shooting would have taken place. (Lake City–Columbia County Historical Museum.)

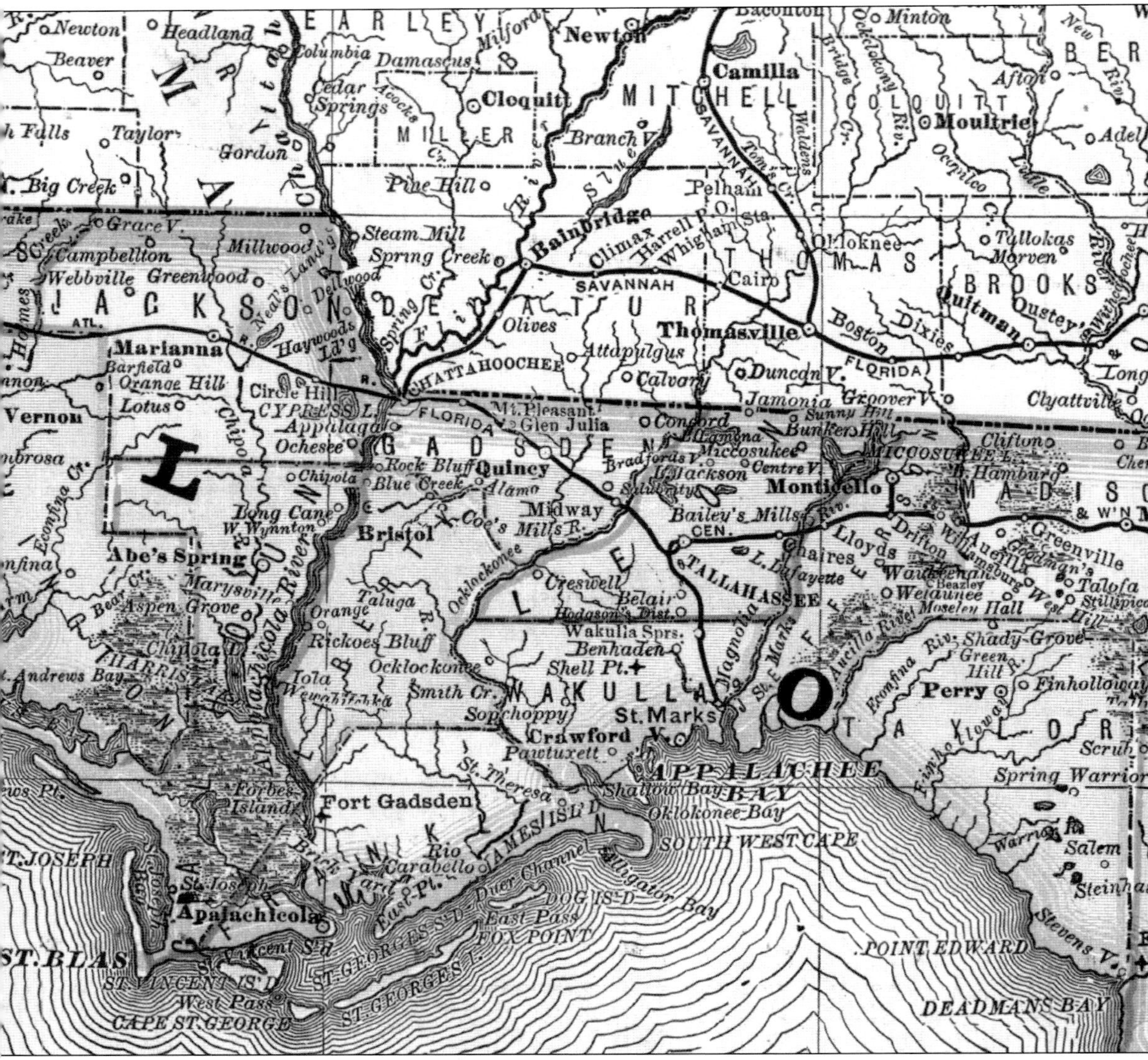

In December 1858, an act was passed in the Florida legislature to change the name of Alligator to Lake City. It was approved by Gov. Madison Perry on January 5, 1859. The most credible reason for the name change is that residents of the area took great pride in its numerous lakes. Also, the Seminole Wars were still in living memory at the time, and having the town named after a Seminole chief did not sit well with some of the residents. Another reason involves a story about a Mrs. Ross, who lobbied for the change because she did not want her daughter to be bullied at

school because she was from a town named Alligator. Lastly, Mayor Matthew Whit Smith's wife, Martha, said she would not hang up her lace curtains in a town called Alligator. A portion of H.H. Hardesty's 1881 map of Florida is seen here, with the present-day shape of Columbia County in the center. (State Archives of Florida.)

The Florida Atlantic & Gulf Central Railroad was chartered in 1851. On March 13, 1860, the railroad opened, running west out of Jacksonville to Lake City. The first locomotive to arrive was the *Jacksonville*, on March 15. In November 1861, the Pensacola & Georgia Railroad was completed, linking Lake City with Tallahassee. This photograph shows railroad workers with a steam locomotive in Lake City around 1900. (State Archives of Florida.)

Silas Niblack was born on March 17, 1825, in Camden County, Georgia. He was admitted to the bar in 1851 and practiced law in Columbia County. He married Atalie Scarborough, daughter of early Alligator pioneer Sterling Scarborough, and was president of the Florida Atlantic & Gulf Central. On March 4, 1868, Niblack sold the railroad due to financial difficulties to William E. Jackson and Associates for $110,000. The railroad was then incorporated as the Florida Central Railroad Company. Silas Niblack died in 1883 at 57 and is buried in the Scarborough Cemetery on Baya Avenue. (State Archives of Florida.)

Two

Faith and Community

Constituted in 1856, First Presbyterian Church was a frame structure in the vicinity of present-day downtown Lake City. The first pastor of the church was Rev. Brazile Leneau. This letter to Reverend Myers of the Presbyterian church in St. Augustine shows an Alligator postmark dated 1857. (State Archives of Florida.)

Around 1888, a new church was constructed near the original church at the corner of South Columbia Avenue and West Nassau Street. This photograph shows the second First Presbyterian Church in the 1880s. The second church was partially destroyed in a fire in 1939 and was eventually demolished. The congregation moved to a new location one mile west of downtown Lake City. (State Archives of Florida.)

The First Advent Church was initially next to the Duncan-Herlong House on Duval Street. Like previous churches that were once in downtown Lake City, the present-day congregation of First Advent Church was moved two miles south on State Route 47. South on the same road, and not too far from First Advent Church, are several churches that were not first established in downtown Lake City, such as the Church of Christ, Christian Heritage Church, Lake City Church of Nazarene, Lake City Baptist Temple, and New Life Outreach Ministries. (Tom and Sue Rowand collection, Dr. Christopher M. Esing.)

The St. James Parish was organized in 1870 with a congregation of 80. In 1880, a church was built and was consecrated by Bishop Young in 1884. In 1898, the parish moved from its location on Alachua Street to Brown Lane and South Marion Avenue, as seen here. In 1898, a rectory was built next to the church, and in 1900, a school was constructed between the buildings. A parish hall was erected in 1926. St. James was recognized by the Episcopal Diocese of Florida in 1960. In 1969, the church purchased a 10-acre property at the intersection of McFarlane Avenue and Brown Lane in addition to an adjacent lot. Instead of building a new church at this location, the church decided to move all of the buildings in August 1987. The church buildings were picked up, placed on flatbed trucks, and moved to their present-day location. (Dr. Christopher M. Esing.)

This photograph shows a First Baptist Church Sunday school class in 1888. From left to right are (first row) Carrie Roberts, Lonnie Sheppard, and May Vinzant; (second row) Lou Jones, Tom C. Chalker (teacher), Vida Barnett, and Bertha Edge; (third row) Edith Knight, Belle McFarlane, Rose Douglass, and Nina Roberts. (State Archives of Florida.)

Constituted in 1869, First Baptist Church was incorporated in 1893. It was originally on the southern end of Olustee Park by Duval Street in a wooden building, which was replaced by the redbrick structure seen here. In 1925, a Colonial-style building, with 48 art glass windows and a pipe organ, was established on Justice Street, which still stands today. (Lake City–Columbia County Historical Museum.)

First Methodist Church was constituted around 1840 in a frame building on Marion Avenue and Dade Street. In 1887, a new frame building was constructed. In 1907, a cement block structure, with two steeples and art glass windows, was constructed on Orange Street and Columbia Avenue, as seen here. A Sunday school building, along with a building called Wesley Hall, was erected in 1926. In 1950, the cement church was demolished, and a new building, called Children's Education, was erected on the same location. (Tom and Sue Rowand collection, Dr. Christopher M. Esing.)

The congregation of First Methodist established a new church building and chapel (Summers Chapel) on Alachua Street, dedicated on September 17, 1950. On May 11, 1967, a fire erupted at the church, Summers Chapel, and the Children's Education Building and destroyed all the structures. A new Methodist church was constructed a mile down Marion Avenue from the original location; its first service was on Palm Sunday in 1970. (Laura Ruth Norris.)

Fort White Methodist Church was established in 1859 at the original Fort White location on the Santa Fe River. When the railroad was built in the town, the church relocated to its present-day site. The 1896 Cedar Keys hurricane destroyed the church, but it was rebuilt in 1897. (Author's collection.)

Trinity United Methodist Church was established in 1863 as Gethsemane Methodist Episcopal Church. The earliest known pastor of the church was Rev. Peter McCray in 1877. The original church burned down in 1925. The present church, seen here, was built in 1927 on Martin Luther King Jr. Street. (Author's collection.)

The Bethel United Methodist Church congregation, or Old Bethel, was established by the early settlers of Alligator around 1824. The original church was a log building two miles north of the present church. In 1856, the congregation had a new church built on land donated by Stephen Sparkman, later referred to as "the white church by the side of the road." (Author's collection.)

In 1865, Father Hugon came to Lake City and had a church built on the corner of Columbia Avenue and Orange Street. In 1944, the Lake City Mission was recognized as a parish. Fr. Michael Kelly was the first Catholic chaplain, and under his direction, Epiphany Catholic Church had a presence at the local VA hospital. The present-day location of Epiphany Catholic Church and Epiphany Catholic School was established in 1955 when the diocese purchased the property. Construction on the church started in 1959 and was completed in 1966; on December 24, 1966, Mass was celebrated in the new church for the first time. In 1959, the Irish Sisters of Mercy opened Epiphany Catholic School. (Rita Swisher.)

Christian Fellowship Church, previously known as Mountaintop Ministries Worldwide, Meade Ministries, and End Time Ministries, found notoriety under the leadership of founder Charles Meade. In 1984, Meade moved to Lake City because of its pristine spring waters, mild temperatures, and rural landscape. The name End Time Ministries led townspeople to believe Meade was leading his followers toward the "end of time." Locals dubbed church members "End Timers." Since Meade's death in 2010, the church made drastic changes to its cultlike atmosphere. Today, the nondenominational congregation occupies this enormous worship center. Current pastor Mark Cady says, "Although the gospel was preached, I'll admit there were some radical teachings. Our ministry now focuses on salvation through a relationship with Jesus Christ." He adds, "Everyone is welcome." (Christian Fellowship Church.)

Three

Civil War

As the Civil War raged in 1863, shortages of food and resources started to hamper the Confederate armies. Florida had the supplies needed to help alleviate some of the hardships endured by the Confederate armies of P.G.T. Beauregard and Braxton Bragg. The Union had occupied nearby Jacksonville for the majority of the war, and launched an invasion of the interior of Florida from there. The purpose of the Union invasion, as outlined by Gen. Quincy Gillmore, was to disrupt Confederate resources, recruit slaves for the Union army, and take Tallahassee. The Union army in Jacksonville, commanded by Gen. Truman Seymour (pictured), ended up marching all the way from Jacksonville to a lake called Ocean Pond, 10 miles east of Lake City. At Ocean Pond, the largest Civil War battle in Florida took place, the Battle of Olustee, which was named after a nearby creek. (Library of Congress.)

Lake City became a base for Confederate general Joseph Finegan, pictured here. He formed the bulk of his army here to encounter the advancing Union army of Truman Seymour. General Beauregard sent Confederate reinforcements to help bolster Finegan's army to meet the impending threat. On February 20, 1864, the Confederate army under General Finegan clashed at Ocean Pond, near Olustee Creek. The Union's advance into the interior of Florida was stopped here. The Union army retreated to Jacksonville and continued to occupy the city for the remainder of the war. (Library of Congress.)

Epaminondas Brown was born in Columbia County on April 29, 1841, to Eliza and Robert Brown. He served in the 4th Florida Infantry in the Civil War. After the war, he was a retail merchant and held many offices in the county. In Blounts Ferry, he was a farmer and postmaster. (MaryAnn Teal.)

Dr. James Hamilton Hill was born on September 13, 1819, in Monroe County, Georgia. Hill attended the Medical College of South Carolina and graduated in 1841. He moved to Columbia County in 1855 with his wife, Martha Thomas, whom he married in 1844. In Columbia County, Hill practiced medicine and farmed. He enlisted in the 3rd Regiment of the Florida Volunteer Infantry on August 10, 1861, as a surgeon. On January 25, 1862, He resigned from service and returned to Lake City. (Harold Murphy.)

Washington Mackey Ives was born on September 29, 1843, in St. Augustine. In 1845, his family moved to Alligator. In 1862, at 18, Ives enlisted in the Confederate army in Company C of the 4th Florida Infantry. After the war, he returned to Lake City and studied law. Ives was elected mayor of Lake City in 1875 and then became a Columbia County judge in 1877. (State Archives of Florida.)

Walter Raleigh Moore was born in Leon County in 1835 to Joseph and Elpenice Moore. The family relocated to Tampa in the 1840s, and around 1852, Walter came to Columbia County, where he engaged in the mercantile industry. During the Civil War, he became a colonel of the 2nd Florida Infantry and was sent to Virginia in July 1861. Colonel Moore was wounded at Seven Pines, Chancellorsville, and Gettysburg and became a prisoner of war on July 2, 1863, at Gettysburg. He was transferred to the prison camp at Johnson's Island in Ohio and remained there until October 11, 1864, when he was exchanged. After the war, Moore returned to Columbia County. From 1881 to 1883, he represented the county in the state House of Representatives. In 1895, accompanied by Col. David Lang, Maj. William Robbins, Col. John Nicholson, and Capt. William Ballantine, he returned to the Gettysburg battlefield. Moore died in Wellborn on October 9, 1898, at the age of 66. This daguerreotype of Moore was taken in the 1860s. (Sue Moody.)

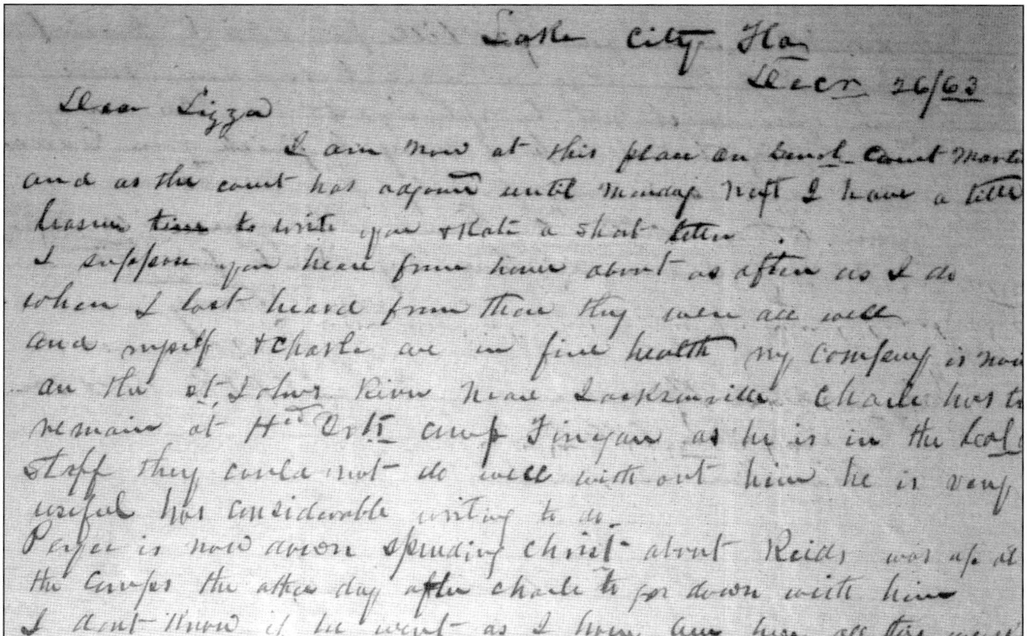

Lake City Fla
Decr 26/63

Dear Lizza

I am now at this place on Genl Court Marti[al]
and as the court has adjourned until monday next I have a little
leasure time to write you & Kate a short letter.
I suppose you hear from home about as often as I do
when I last heard from them they were all well
and myself & Charlie are in fine health my company is now
on the St Johns River near Jacksonville Charlie has to
remain at Hd Qrts camp Finegan as he is in the [illegible]
staff they could not do well with out him he is very
useful has considerable writing to do.
[illegible] is now [illegible] spending christ[mas] about Reids was up at
the camps the other day after Charlie to go down with him
I dont know if he went as I have been here all this week

This is a portion of Capt. John Pearson's letter to his daughter Eliza, written December 26, 1863, in Lake City. In the letter, Pearson tells Eliza his company was at Camp Finegan near the St. Johns River in Jacksonville and is now at Lake City. Pearson took part in the Battle of Olustee in February 1864, two months later. (Author's collection.)

The house of Louise Cathy was converted into a hospital for Union and Confederate wounded from the Battle of Olustee. Louise Cathy cared for soldiers from both sides because it was her duty as a Christian to render aid to everyone. Probably located at the corner of Railroad Street and Marion Avenue, the house was most likely burned down. (State Archives of Florida.)

Around 620,000 people, or roughly two percent of the nation's population, lost their lives in the Civil War. The majority of deaths were due to disease. This sketch by student Edward Powers shows a Lake City schoolhouse that served as a hospital during the war. (University of Florida.)

The Cline Barfield House, on the right, was the first brick house in Lake City. This 1883 photograph was taken near East Davis Street. George Cline, who served in the Confederate army during the Civil War, was the first owner of the house. While he was serving, his wife, Julia, and son John assisted in caring for the wounded from the Battle of Olustee. Because John Cline had assisted in caring for the wounded in 1864, he was granted a pension in 1955 when his health was in decline. (Lake City–Columbia County Historical Museum.)

The Confederate dead from the Battle of Olustee were buried in Lake City at Oaklawn Cemetery. The Confederates who were wounded were brought to Lake City, where they either died from their wounds, died from disease, or were transferred to another city. On February 14, 2014, a sesquicentennial memorial was placed at Oak Lawn Cemetery in memory of the Confederate dead interred at the cemetery. (State Archives of Florida.)

In downtown Lake City, a Battle of Olustee memorial was established on January 28, 1928, at Olustee Park. From left to right are Col. Thomas Jefferson Appleyard, US Army chief of staff Maj. Gen. Charles Pelot Summerall, Virginia Phillips, Florida state senator William W. Phillips, Robert McColskey, and Gov. John Martin. (State Archives of Florida.)

Olustee Park was called City Park in the early 1900s. The Columbia County Courthouse occupied the present-day park until 1902, when the new courthouse was built adjacent to the park. This postcard shows Olustee Park in the 1930s. The bandstand was in a different location then. (State Archives of Florida.)

In 1897, the United Daughters of the Confederacy decided to raise funds for a memorial at the Battle of Olustee site. The Florida legislature established a commission in 1899 to oversee the memorial. The memorial was dedicated on October 23, 1912, with Battle of Olustee veterans participating in the ceremony. (State Archives of Florida.)

During Reconstruction, several Springfield Model 1868 rifles were taken from the Union forces that had been occupying Lake City since the end of the Civil War and thrown into Lake DeSoto to protest their presence in the city. In December 1982, sixteen of these rifles were recovered from the lake when it was drained. Some of the rifles are seen here at the Lake City–Columbia County Historical Museum. (Author's collection.)

The first Battle of Olustee reenactment took place in 1977. This flyer advertised the second reenactment the following year. In 1979, interest grew, and an organization called the Blue-Grey Army was established to support and raise funds for the reenactment by holding activities in Lake City. The Olustee Festival in Lake City started in the early 1980s, and since then, it has become linked to the Battle of Olustee reenactment. (State Archives of Florida.)

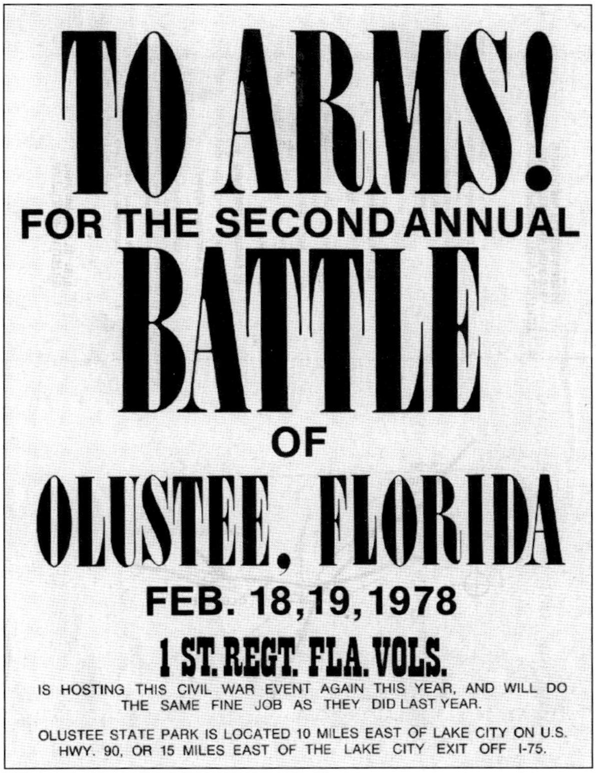
TO ARMS!
FOR THE SECOND ANNUAL
BATTLE
OF
OLUSTEE, FLORIDA
FEB. 18,19,1978
1 ST. REGT. FLA. VOLS.
IS HOSTING THIS CIVIL WAR EVENT AGAIN THIS YEAR, AND WILL DO THE SAME FINE JOB AS THEY DID LAST YEAR.
OLUSTEE STATE PARK IS LOCATED 10 MILES EAST OF LAKE CITY ON U.S. HWY. 90, OR 15 MILES EAST OF THE LAKE CITY EXIT OFF I-75.

The Olustee Festival is an annual event in downtown Lake City. Venders, events, and shows are hosted in the vicinity of Olustee Park. The annual Olustee Festival parade is also held downtown. This 2019 photograph shows the beginning of the parade at the VA hospital; participants are marching north toward Olustee Park. (Author's collection.)

This photograph shows the reenactment of the Battle of Olustee at Lake DeSoto in 2019. Not seen is the reenactment of the battle of the *Monitor* and *Merrimack* happening nearby on Lake DeSoto. This naval battle actually took place near Norfolk, Virginia, but the reenactment was incorporated into the annual reenactment of the Battle of Olustee. (Author's collection.)

John Vinzant Jr. was born in Tatnall County, Georgia, in 1840. His father, John Vinzant Sr., moved his family to Florida and settled in Columbia County. During the Civil War, Vinzant Jr. enlisted in Company A, 1st Florida Cavalry, under Gen. Kirby Smith. On December 4, 1864, he had his right leg shot off near Murfreesboro, Tennessee. After the war, he relocated to Columbia County. Vinzant Jr. became a store clerk and a teacher until 1877. He met Mattie Futch in 1871 when her parents went to the store where he was working. They were married on January 29, 1874, and had three children: Martha, May, and Birdie. John Vinzant Jr. was appointed clerk of the circuit court for Columbia County and moved to Lake City in 1877. He continued to teach part-time, and served on the board of trustees of the Lake City Institute. In 1880, he bought his house for $450. He served for 16 years as clerk of the court and two years as tax collector. (Lake City–Columbia County Historical Museum.)

May Vinzant Perkins was the daughter of John Vinzant Jr. and became one of Lake City's first historians. In 1909, she married Herbert Perkins in Jacksonville. May Perkins took ownership of her father's house after his death in 1907, and owned it until her death in 1981 at the age of 102; she was one of only a few local centenarians. (Vinzant/Livingstone Collection.)

The house of May Perkins, seen here in the 1930s, has been referred to as the May Vinzant Perkins house since her death in 1981. In 1982, locals organized the Historic Preservation Board of Lake City and Columbia County Inc. In October 1983, the board and the Blue-Grey Army Inc. jointly agreed to buy the May Vinzant Perkins house. The two groups restored the house to serve as a historical and cultural center as well as a museum and headquarters for the Blue-Grey Army and the board. The result of this is the Lake City–Columbia County Historical Museum Board, which is today's Lake City–Columbia County Historical Museum. The museum annually participates in the Battle of Olustee Festival and has a variety of Civil War and local historical items. (Vinzant/Livingstone Collection.)

Four

College City

Passed in 1862 during the Civil War, the Morrill Land-Grant Act allowed grants of land to the states for the establishment of colleges in agriculture and mechanical arts. The Florida legislature chartered the Florida Agricultural College in 1870. The first site chosen for the school was at Eau Gallie in Melbourne, Brevard County. Construction was started in 1876, but it was never opened due to political problems, and in 1882, the trustees of the college instead offered to relocate it. Columbia County citizens headed by Joseph Baya the namesake of present-day Baya Drive, offered 112 acres to the college. The land was part of Baya's homestead. Columbia County offered an immediate $1,000 to get construction underway. A $15,000 subsidy was obtained from the land grant fund to cover salaries and other expenses. In February 1883, Lake City was chosen as the site for the college, and classes began in the fall of 1884. This photograph shows Florida Agricultural College cadets in uniform in the 1890s. (University of Florida.)

This 1893 photograph shows the faculty of Florida Agricultural College. Courses included physics, mathematics, chemistry, business, French, Spanish, and biology. The classes revolved around military programs. The school's creed of 1901 begins, "We believe that we are the best educational institution in the State."

The curriculum at Florida Agricultural College included agricultural training and military programs. The college was first opened to white males until becoming a coeducational institution in 1893. Students resided in dormitories, and daily chapel and Sunday worship at a church of the student's choice were required. This photograph shows female cadets on the steps of Chapel Hall. (University of Florida.)

A student is working in the machinery shop at Florida Agricultural College in the 1890s. In 1901, the enrollment was 51, with a faculty of 19. Military discipline was the main focus at the college, and students took courses in a variety of subjects, like woodworking. Half of the students were from Lake City. (University of Florida.)

In 1901, Henry Flagler, founder of the Florida East Coast Railway and cofounder of Standard Oil, donated $10,000 to the school for a gymnasium. In 1903, the Florida legislature changed the name of Florida Agriculture College to the University of Florida. The gymnasium became a noteworthy addition to the campus, and the new name seemed to indicate a promising future for the school, but unfortunately, it was not to be. This postcard shows the Flagler gymnasium in the 1910s when it was part of Columbia College. (Tom and Sue Rowand collection, Dr. Christopher M. Esing.)

Florida in 1905 was funding many colleges in the state and could not maintain so many institutions, such as the University of Florida at Lake City. Gov. Napoleon Broward, along with the state legislature, considered plans for consolidation. In Tallahassee, the state board of education in a joint session voted to move the University of Florida from Lake City to Gainesville. This building was later used as part of the VA hospital. (State Archives of Florida.)

The citizens of Lake City were unhappy with the decision to move the university to Gainesville and mourned the loss of their school. In the summer of 1906, the move to Gainesville began but not without problems. Anger among the local citizens led to threats of violence when University of Florida equipment started to move out of town. Professor Cawthon carried a loaded rifle and oversaw the removal of items just in case there were any signs of violence. The loss of the University of Florida was a deep blow to the citizens of Lake City. (State Archives of Florida.)

The Lake City Institute was on Lake DeSoto next to First Baptist Church. It opened in 1888 as a private school for women. J.B. Edge, Joseph H. Porter, K.D. Edge, John Vinzant, J.M. Futch, T.S. Chalker, W.R. Chalker, J.O. Harris, M.F. Brown, and the First Baptist Church helped establish the institute. Reverend Drew of the First Baptist Church was the first principal. The institute closed in 1893 when the Florida Agricultural College became a coeducational institution. This photograph of Lake City Institute is from 1892. (State Archives of Florida.)

After Lake City lost the University of Florida to Gainesville in 1906 and the Lake City Institute closed in 1893 due to the Florida Agricultural College, the town hoped to regain a college to fill the void left behind. The abandoned campus of the University of Florida covered 335 acres. It was forfeited to the state under the supervision of the Florida Board of Education, and in 1907, Lake City conveyed some of the land to the Florida Baptist Convention. The Baptists, who operated the Lake City Institute, leased the buildings and grounds from Lake City and created Columbia College in 1907. The college was also referred to as the Baptist State College of Florida in advertisements. (State Archives of Florida.)

Columbia College operated as a private, church-affiliated, coed institution for 10 years until 1917, when it merged with Stetson University in Deland. During World War I, the campus was occupied by the Florida militia. After the war, the campus was returned to Lake City. On May 20, 1920, ownership of the former Columbia College and University of Florida campus was transferred to the federal government. This photograph shows the state champion Columbia College baseball team in 1912. (H. Morris Williams Collection.)

After 1917, Lake City was without a higher education institution for 30 years until the creation of the Columbia Forestry School on the former Naval Air Station Lake City property in 1947. The school struggled with enrollment and funding for the first few years, which led the president to ask for assistance from the Florida legislature. The University of Florida took over management of the school in 1950, and it was renamed the University of Florida Forest Ranger School. The photograph above shows the Columbia Forestry School around 1948. Below is a class at the Forest Ranger School in the 1950s. (Above, Lake City Chamber of Commerce; below, Florida Gateway College.)

In 1962, the Forest Ranger School became part of the Florida network of community schools and was renamed Lake City Junior College and Forest Ranger School. This photograph shows Hayden Burns, governor of Florida from 1965 to 1967, delivering a speech at the college in 1966. (Florida Gateway College.)

The Lake City Junior College and Forest Ranger School had fewer than 400 students in the 1960s. Forest and timber technology courses were some of the programs offered by the college. The location of the college near Osceola National Forest made it an ideal place for such programs. The sign in this photograph was about five miles from what is considered to be the boundary of the national forest. (Florida Gateway College.)

In 1970, Lake City Junior College was renamed Lake City Community College, seen here in the 1970s. Florida Agricultural College was in Lake City for 22 years, and Lake City Community College has now exceeded that. (Florida Gateway College.)

After a fire destroyed several buildings in 1963, wooden buildings were replaced with brick. In 2010, Lake City Community College was renamed Florida Gateway College. It has three satellite branches in Cross City, Bell, and Olustee. The Olustee branch is the Public Service Training Campus, which is used for EMS, firefighter, law enforcement, and corrections training. This photograph shows the main campus filled with pine trees and a sculpture of timber wolves, the school's mascot. (Florida Gateway College.)

Wilson Samuel Rivers was a Lake Butler native, born in 1922. In 1940, he attended the University of Florida and earned a bachelor's degree in business administration. In World War II, Rivers served as a first lieutenant in the Infantry in the Pacific. After the war, he returned to his hometown where he purchased his father's gristmill in 1947, running it himself for the next 40 years. Rivers became a volunteer fireman, tree farmer, and chairman of the board of the Lake City Community College for 28 years. Construction on a new library for the Florida Gateway College began in 2009. In 2011, Rivers died at the age of 89. The Wilson S. Rivers Library & Media Center, seen here in 2019, was opened in 2012. (Author's collection.)

Five

Armed Forces and Law Enforcement

In 1917, the buildings of the former Florida Agricultural College and University of Florida were briefly used by Company C of the 1st Florida Infantry during World War I. After the war, the buildings were vacant. On May 20, 1920, the buildings and land were transferred to the federal government and converted into the US Health Service Hospital No. 63. In 1924, the hospital was renamed Veterans Bureau Hospital No. 63. In 1930, it became the Lake City US Veterans Administration Hospital. This postcard of the VA hospital is from the 1930s. (Tom and Sue Rowand collection, Dr. Christopher M. Esing.)

The Science Hall of Florida Agricultural College is seen here in the early 1900s. The building was used as the surgical wing of the VA hospital until it was demolished in 1956. Buildings of the former college were used for the hospital until they became inadequate in the mid-20th century. (State Archives of Florida.)

The original buildings of the former University of Florida were all demolished and are no longer part of the VA hospital. The present-day hospital can be seen in this postcard from 1967. Due to the growing need of medical care for veterans, the hospital became an important institution for Lake City. (State Archives of Florida.)

On April 21, 1898, the United States declared war on Spain in response to the sinking of the USS *Maine* in Havana Harbor. The Spanish-American War ended with the signing of the Treaty of Paris on December 10, 1898, in which Spain ceded Puerto Rico and Guam. The Philippines were also ceded to the United States for $20 million. This 1898 photograph shows Columbia County volunteers from the Spanish-American War. The civilian in the back is John Dudley Crabb Sr., and the boy in the front is his son Roy Crabb. (State Archives of Florida.)

Gen. Charles Pelot Summerall was the most prominent military leader from Columbia County, born in Blounts Ferry on March 4, 1867. From 1882 to 1885, he attended the Porter Military Academy in South Carolina and then West Point in 1888. After graduating from West Point in 1892, he served in the Spanish-American War and the Philippine-American War. From 1905 to 1911, he was the senior instructor of artillery tactics at West Point. During World War I, he commanded the 1st Infantry Division in France. From 1926 to 1930, Summerall was the chief of staff of the US Army. He is seen here (right) with Secretary of War James W. Good during Army Day, April 6, 1929. (Library of Congress.)

In 1934, Lake City citizens created a flying club and an airfield that eventually led to two small runways east of the city. In 1942, the US Navy took ownership of the runways and constructed a larger airfield. Naval Air Station Lake City was commissioned on December 8, 1942, as one of 11 naval air stations in Florida. This photograph shows an engineering hangar at Lake City in 1944. (Lake City Chamber of Commerce.)

The naval air station orchestra is seen playing at the Women's Club in 1944. The station's logo, seen here, was a duck holding onto a rope attached to two airplane engines. The Women's Club was used by the United Service Organization to entertain members of the armed forces during the war. (Lake City Chamber of Commerce.)

In January 1943, Operational Training Unit VB-2 No. 2 at Naval Air Station Jacksonville began training at Naval Air Station Lake City with the Lockheed PV-1 Ventura and Lockheed PBO Hudson airplanes. Lake City trained pilots and assisted with Jacksonville operations. This photograph shows a Lake City traffic control tower in 1944. (Lake City Chamber of Commerce.)

At one time, Naval Air Station Lake City had 294 officers, 1,128 enlisted men, and 266 civilians. It had four asphalt runways, with the number of aircraft peaking at 80 in 1945. There was an assembly and repair department to assist with aircraft maintenance. This photograph shows several US Army Air Forces pilots at the station. Lake City operated until March 1946, when operations transferred to Hutchinson, Kansas, and Whiting Field, Florida. (Lake City Chamber of Commerce, Dr. Christopher M. Esing.)

A pilot from Naval Air Station Lake City is greeting Lake City children near the Columbia County tax collector's building and the Lake City Chamber of Commerce. The area is now a parking lot for visitors to Olustee Park. (Lake City–Columbia County Chamber of Commerce, Dr. Christopher M. Esing.)

The Columbia County unit that served in World War II was Company H of the 124th Infantry, mobilized in 1940. Company H trained at Camp Blanding and then at the Infantry School in Fort Benning, Georgia. The 124th Infantry was sent to the Pacific and fought in the Philippines and New Guinea. Several other Columbia County citizens fought in Europe. A memorial at Olustee Park is dedicated to the 40 soldiers from Columbia County who died in World War II. This photograph shows World War II veterans participating in the 2017 Veterans Day parade in downtown Lake City. (Author's collection.)

Robert Henry Jenkins Jr. was born on June 1, 1948, in Interlachen, Florida. In 1967, he graduated from Central Academy in Palatka, Florida, and completed Marine Corps training in 1968. Jenkins was assigned to the 3rd Reconnaissance Battalion, 3rd Marine Division in Vietnam in July 1968. On March 5, 1969, at Firebase Argonne, Jenkins, along with a recon team, was attacked. While Jenkins and Fred Ostrom took up positions to return fire, a hand grenade was thrown at them. Jenkins jumped onto Ostrom, shielding him from the blast, and was mortally wounded. Jenkins's sacrifice to save his fellow Marine earned him the Medal of Honor posthumously. The Robert H. Jenkins Jr. Domiciliary Home in Lake City is named in his honor. At Olustee Park, there is a Vietnam War memorial dedicated to 23 Columbia County natives who lost their lives in the war. (State Archives of Florida.)

William Thurston Strange was the grandson of Thomas Strange, the first Confederate soldier to be killed in Florida during the Civil War. William Strange was the town marshal of Lake City from 1890 to 1892. He was killed in the line of duty in 1900 at 32 years old. His tombstone reads, "Gave his life in defense of law and order." (State Archives of Florida.)

The Lake City Police Department started around 1861, during the Civil War. Colonel House was the first police chief, from 1861 to 1865. Here is an early photograph of the Lake City Police Department. From left to right are officer O.S. Moore Sr., unidentified, Chief Charlie Eaton, officer Jeff Hunt, and officer George Douglas Sr. (State Archives of Florida.)

Wiley Albertus "Babe" Douglass, also known as W.B. Douglass, was born on August 7, 1885, in Starke, Florida. In 1885, the Douglass family moved to Lake City, where Babe was raised. He attended the Peabody Institute and worked at the Seaboard Railway and in the turpentine industry in Ocala. In the 1910s, he returned to Lake City and held many offices, such as chief of police, constable, and city commissioner. From 1922 to 1933, he was the sheriff of Lake City. The photograph of Babe Douglass was taken in 1915. (State Archives of Florida.)

In 1958, the Lake City council approved the purchase of the state road department building to be used for city hall and the police department. In 1967, the old city hall was remodeled with a new police department and jail. In 2004, a new building for the Lake City Police Department was built on Main Boulevard, seen here. The old city hall building has since been demolished. (Author's collection.)

Six

Columbia County Schools

The Peabody Institute started in 1889 with courses in algebra, geography, history, Latin, and penmanship. Pictured here are students from the Peabody Institute in 1890. The school was on West St. Johns Street. At the bottom of the photograph is an arrow pointing to Babe Douglass, future sheriff of Lake City. (State Archives of Florida.)

Here is the seventh-grade class of Columbia Graded and High School in 1910. Mattie O'Neal was the teacher, and John Barnett is at far right. The building in the back is the present-day city hall of Lake City. The building at right center behind the trees is the Chalker residence, which is now a parking lot. (H. Morris Williams Collection.)

The Peabody Institute, later called the Peabody Graded and High School, was the predecessor of Columbia High School. In 1893, the school relocated to West Duval Street and was renamed Columbia Graded and High School. The first Columbia High School was a wooden structure used from 1893 to 1906. (State Archives of Florida.)

Columbia High School started one of the first football programs in Florida, in 1911. This is the 1922 Columbia High football team. Columbia football has become an important part of Lake City and Columbia County. The Tigers won regional championships in 1969, 1998, and 2003. In 1967, the Tigers, coached by Paul Quinn, won the 1967 state championship. (H. Morris Williams Collection.)

Memorial Stadium was used for Columbia High School's football team from 1923 to 1993. This photograph of the stadium is from the 1970s. Since 1994, the Columbia Tigers play at Columbia High School Tiger Stadium. Memorial Stadium is still used for local events. (Lake City Chamber of Commerce, Dr. Christopher M. Esing.)

The third Columbia High School is pictured in 1928. The school was built in 1921 as Columbia County's only high school and was used from 1923 to 1959. When it reached capacity in 1957, a new school was built on Pennsylvania Avenue. The third Columbia High School building was converted into Lake City Junior High School in the 1970s. After Lake City Middle School was built in 1990, the second Columbia High School building was then used for the Columbia County School District administration. (State Archives of Florida.)

Here is a 1960s aerial photograph of the fourth Columbia High School on Pennsylvania Avenue. Alligator Lake is behind the school. In 1975, Columbia High School moved to its current location on State Route 441. The present-day Columbia High School includes a gymnasium, soccer fields, tennis courts, and a football stadium. The former Columbia High School is now Richardson Sixth Grade Academy. (H. Morris Williams Collection.)

Richardson High School was built in 1957 for local African American students on present-day Coach Anders Lane. The Richardson Wolves excelled in basketball and football, winning the 1967–1968 state basketball championship. This photograph shows the 1956 Wolves football team. The school closed in the 1970s after integration. The majority of the school building was demolished except for the cafeteria and gym. The gym and the former playing fields are now part of the Richardson Community Center. (H. Morris Williams Collection.)

The first Fort White High School was built in 1915, and an auditorium was added in 1936. The class of 1969 was the last to graduate from this school building. From 1969 to 2000, Fort White did not have a school due to not having enough students in the area. Since the first Fort White High School closed in 1969, students from Fort White were sent to Columbia High School in Lake City. By 2000, the population of Fort White and the surrounding areas grew and there was a need for a new school. The present Fort White High School was built in 2000, with the first class graduating in 2001. The original school still stands as of 2020. (Author's collection.)

Five Points is a community immediately north of Lake City. The name comes from the five roads that come together at US Route 441, making five points at the intersection. One of the five roads is Gum Swamp Road, which goes to the Big Gum Swamp Wilderness. This photograph shows Five Points Elementary School in 1956. The school has been in Five Points since 1955. (H. Morris Williams Collection.)

Alfonso Levy is directing the Niblack Elementary School band. Niblack Elementary was established in 1954 to consolidate Columbia County elementary schools serving African American students. The school is named after principal, teacher, and county supervisor Minnie J. Niblack, who worked to improve and consolidate schools in Columbia County. (State Archives of Florida.)

Mason City is 11 miles south of Lake City near Mount Tabor. The Mason City School was consolidated in 1924. In 1928–1929, the school became a senior high school. The Mason City Community Center now stands at the location of the former school. (State Archives of Florida.)

The Winfield School and students are seen in 1896. Principal A.W. Jackson is standing at far left, and teacher Addie Edmonson is sitting in the center of the second row. The schoolhouse was used by Falling Creek Methodist Church for its services. Winfield is in the vicinity of Falling Creek Falls. (State Archives of Florida.)

Watertown Public School first opened in 1938 in the Watertown area east of Lake City. This photograph of the school was taken around 1975. The school bell was moved to Eastside Elementary in 1959 and then to the Columbia County School District building in 2001. (Lake City Chamber of Commerce, Dr. Christopher M. Esing.)

Seven

Faces and Places of Modern Columbia County

This 1920 photograph shows cousins P.G. Harrington (left) and Julian Parrott with an ox and cart at the Harrington homestead. Oxen were used around farms until trucks became common. In the background at right is a birdhouse and gourds for swallows. (State Archives of Florida.)

Pictured is the Edward Henry Robarts family in front of their house in Lake City around 1910. In the photograph are Mary Esther Robarts Sheppard, Edward Henry Robarts, Mysetta W. Robarts, Edward Oswald Robarts, Ruby Robarts Keefe, Marcus Ralph Robarts, George Washington "Wash" Robarts, and Irma Robarts Kinnard. (State Archives of Florida.)

Here is a picture of Holdsworth family members at the Thompson home in the 1890s. Professor Holdsworth had moved to Lake City to teach at Florida Agricultural College. (Lake City–Columbia County Historical Museum, Dr. Christopher M. Esing.)

Agnes Jones was born a slave in Tatnall County, Georgia, and was brought to Columbia County in 1844 by the Mattox family. After the Civil War, Jones continued to work for the Mattox family. In 1883, she and her husband, Charles, known as Uncle Jenks, bought the property of what is now the Richardson Community Center. Jones built a house and a garden on her property. Over time, she gathered bones and developed a boneyard in her garden. (State Archives of Florida.)

Agnes Jones later went by the name Aunt Aggie, and her boneyard became a popular destination. She charged no admission but did have flowers and vegetables for sale. Aunt Aggie's boneyard was a curious spectacle not just for locals but also for tourists who would come over from the Blanche Hotel to see her creations. Aunt Aggie died in 1918, leaving her property to change hands a number of times until the Columbia County School Board bought it in 1928. The property was razed in 1930 by Marvin Mattox, the grandson of her former owner, and Richardson High School was built on the site. (State Archives of Florida.)

Virgil Waitman was a former slave from Savannah who arrived in Lake City after the Civil War. In Lake City, he was a farmer and was known to everyone as Uncle Virge. He had his own place on Wire Road, now US Route 41. Waitman married Lizzie Williamson, and they had several children. Waitman died in 1928. (State Archives of Florida.)

This early 1900s photograph shows the first telephone in Lake City. The person on the left is Nettie Sheppard, the central operator. In 1900, Lake City was the first city in Florida to have underground wires for a telephone system. (State Archives of Florida.)

The Mathis plow with a hydraulic system was developed by Leon Mathis of Lake City and was used for forest fire protection. The first Mathis plow is at the Smithsonian Institution. The Mathis Welding and Machine Company was created in 1928 to manufacture plows and other forestry equipment. In 1981, the company moved to Starkville, Mississippi, and merged with Forestry Equipment Sales Company to form FESCO. In 2013, Oliver & Dahlman Equipment Company of Hasting, Florida, purchased FESCO. (State Archives of Florida.)

Osceola National Forest was created on July 10, 1931, by Pres. Herbert Hoover. The four largest acquisitions that formed the national forest were Columbia Farms, J.C. Marsh, Ocean Pond Land Company, and E.A. McColskey. The forest is named after Osceola, a Seminole leader in the 1830s during the Seminole Wars. (State Archives of Florida.)

This is a forest ranger vehicle in Osceola National Forest in the 1940s. The forest is an important part of the economy of Lake City and the surrounding counties. It covers part of Hamilton, Bradford, Baker, and Columbia Counties. It includes a wilderness area called the Big Gum Swamp Wilderness, about 21 miles northeast of Lake City. The wilderness area was designated by Congress in 1984. (State Archives of Florida.)

Pictured is a large cypress log on the back of a truck in the 1930s. The lumber industry at this time was centered around Lake City and the nearby mills of Watertown. Shipbuilding materials derived from the resin of pine and coniferous trees, including turpentine, pine oil, rosin, and tar, were valuable products of the Florida lumber industry. (State Archives of Florida.)

Frederick Preston "Fred" Cone was born on September 28, 1871, in Benton to Sarah and William Haddock Cone. He was the grandson of William "Billy" Cone and attended Florida Agricultural College and Jasper Normal College. In 1892, he passed the bar exam despite never having received a law degree. From 1907 to 1912, he was a member of the Florida House of Representatives. In 1912, Fred Cone and other citizens of Lake City established the Columbia County Bank. From 1937 to 1941, Cone was the governor of Florida. In 1939, he created the Florida Highway Patrol. In 1940, he ran for the vacant Senate seat of Park Trammell. Cone was defeated in the Democratic primary by Charles Andrews. He died on July 28, 1948, in Lake City. (State Archives of Florida.)

This photograph shows Lake City and Columbia County citizens going to the Farmers Independent Warehouse around 1940. Tobacco, which was auctioned at the warehouse, became an important crop of Columbia County after World War II. The Farmers Independent Warehouse is now the site of the Columbia County Fairgrounds. (State Archives of Florida.)

Agriculture in Columbia County consisted of cotton, sugarcane, corn, and peas in the pre–Civil War years. After the war, agriculture shifted more to vegetable and fruit cultivation. By 1935, flue-cured burley tobacco used for cigarettes became a dominant crop in the county. This photograph shows a load of leaf tobacco in a burlap sack during an auction at the Farmers Independent Warehouse in 1947. (State Archives of Florida.)

Luther Richards is starting an engine for Florida Power & Light in 1941. The company was established in 1925 and has its headquarters in Juno Beach, Florida. It initially owned power plants, gas plants, water facilities, and ice companies throughout Florida. In the late 1930s, it began to add rural electric lines in smaller communities and provided power to several military bases before World War II. Florida Power & Light had a presence in Columbia County by the 1930s. (State Archives of Florida.)

In 1946, Florida Power & Light added 3,000 miles of rural electric lines in Florida. This photograph shows workers installing power poles in the early 1950s. On the pole are N.E. King and Frank Williamson. Lake City had the first electric lights in Florida, in 1891. (State Archives of Florida.)

R.G. Granger established a lumbermill in Watertown in 1943. The mill would cut about 400 trees a day and averaged over six million feet of timber annually. This photograph shows the lumbermill in 1956. Granger was forced to shut down the mill in 1957 due to other mills purchasing most of the timber in the area and refusing to sell to private mills. Granger's was one of the last privately owned lumbermills in Florida. (State Archives of Florida.)

Watertown Lake is about three miles east of downtown Lake City at the border of Osceola National Forest. This photograph shows the Florida Game and Freshwater Fish Commission preparing to unload fish into the lake in 1964. The name Watertown comes from the community that developed around the mills near the lake in the late 19th and early 20th centuries. The community was comprised of workers and their families living in small houses near the mills. (State Archives of Florida.)

Guerdon Industries had a plant on the property of the former Naval Air Statio Lake City where it assembled mobile homes. This photograph shows a worker constructing a mobile home at the plant in 1963. The starting pay at Guerdon Industries in 1963 was $1.75 per hour, equivalent to $14.70 in 2020. (State Archives of Florida.)

Officials have just unveiled the Lake City turnoff sign on Interstate 75. Gov. Farris Bryant is seen getting in his car at far right. Lake City's position at the intersection of Interstates 75 and 10 transformed the town. (State Archives of Florida.)

Pat Summerall was born in Lake City on May 10, 1930, and attended Columbia High School, playing football, basketball, tennis, and baseball. He attended the University of Arkansas, majoring in Russian history and playing on the Razorbacks football team. After graduating in 1952, Summerall played professional football for the Detroit Lions and was with the team as a placekicker for its second national championship in 1953. From 1953 to 1958, Summerall played for the Chicago Cardinals, and then the New York Giants from 1958 to 1961. In 1962, Summerall began his career as a sportscaster and, from 1981 to 2002, was noted for his sportscasting work with John Madden. (State Archives of Florida.)

Robert Russell "Chubby" Wise was born on October 2, 1915, in Lake City into a musical family. He dropped out of seventh grade and began playing the fiddle around 15. Wise became a famous bluegrass fiddle player, popularizing the song "Orange Blossom Special," and was a member of the Grand Ole Opry. (State Archives of Florida.)

Johnny Cash is seen performing at Lake City Community College in 1982. When Cash was in Lake City, he visited the Perkins House, which at the time was undergoing a transition into the Lake City–Columbia County Historical Museum. Cash stayed with Pat Summerall at his house on Alligator Lake. (Blue-Grey Army and Lake City–Columbia County Historical Museum.)

The Columbia County Fair was started in 1938 by Columbia County Resources Inc. The purpose of the organization was to aid children of the county by holding fairs for the benefit and development of the agriculture, horticulture, and animal husbandry of Columbia County. The fairs were originally called the Slash Pine Forest and Farm Festival. They were not conducted after 1941 due to World War II. In the 1950s, 4-H Club activities renewed interest in the fair, and it was revived in 1957 at Strickland's Tobacco Warehouse. The fair's objective was to promote agriculture and forestry in Columbia County. The revived fair was called the Forestry and Farm Festival until 1960, when it was renamed the Columbia County Fair. It continued to use the tobacco warehouse until new buildings were established in the 1960s at its present location between US Route 90 and State Route 247. (Laura Ruth Norris.)

William Bascom Norris was born on November 15, 1926, in Lake City. His mother, Ethel, died two days after he was born. Throughout his life, he was referred to as Bascom Norris rather than by his first name, William. Due to the death of his mother and absence of his father, Norris was raised by various family members. It was his ideology that drove him to success and giving back to the community. In one instance, Norris, in his youth, pieced together parts from three different bicycles to make one working bicycle so he could make deliveries. In World War II, Norris served in the Navy as a cook. (Laura Ruth Norris.)

Norris's father-in-law, Paul Giebeig Sr., purchased all the land of the Adams brothers in the 1950s, and Norris purchased the eastern portion, totaling around 1,000 acres, in the early 1960s. He saw a need for a road between US Route 90 and US Route 41, and in 1977, he donated a large amount of land from Lake Jeffrey Road to US Route 41. Norris attempted to persuade others to donate land between Lake Jeffrey Road and US Route 90, but had little success. He died in 1992 at 65, but his vision did not die with him. After his death, land was gradually donated, and eventually the road that he had envisioned was created. The county commissioners had to vote on one name for the road and settled on Bascom Norris Drive to honor Norris's vision, his contributions, and his volunteer service as the longest-serving president of the Columbia County Fair Association, from 1972 to 1992. This photograph shows Norris at a ribbon-cutting ceremony for the fair in 1969. (Laura Ruth Norris.)

Lake City's location in North Central Florida has brought in major businesses from out of state, like US Cold Storage and Target. Target established a food distribution center in Lake City in 2007. It was Target's first food distribution center and ships to Target stores throughout the Southeastern United States. (Author's collection.)

Aero Corporation was at the Lake City Airport near Lake City Community College. The company hired over 1,000 residents to work on various aircraft. This photograph shows two employees working on an aircraft in 1965. The Aero Corporation facility in Lake City was later used by TIMCO Aviation Services. In 2014, TIMCO was acquired by Hong Kong Aircraft Engineering Company, which now occupies the current facility. (State Archives of Florida.)

In the late 1970s, Ray Sessions started Cannon Creek Airpark off Sisters Welcome Road as a community for aviation enthusiasts. The airpark was constructed with two runways and is used by neighborhood residents to store their personal aircraft near their homes. This photograph shows an aircraft on loan from the National Museum of Naval Aviation at Cannon Creek Airpark. Sisters Welcome Road is named after the nearby Sisters Welcome Baptist Church, which was constituted in 1899. (Author's collection.)

Eight

DOWNTOWN LAKE CITY

Throughout the history of Columbia County, there have been several courthouses beginning with the cabin of early settler Noel Raulerson. The courthouses that were built in the 19th century were destroyed in 1848, 1860, 1867, and 1874 due to fires. The courthouse built in 1874 in the center of present-day Olustee Park was the first to not be destroyed by fire. When plans for the present-day courthouse were made around 1900, the 1874 courthouse was disassembled. The house on West De Soto Street seen here was built using the disassembled pieces. (Tom and Sue Rowand collection, Dr. Christopher M Esing.)

This panoramic view of downtown Lake City in 1885 shows Lake DeSoto and Lake Isabella near downtown. The large lake in the back is Lake Hamburg, also known as Lake Montgomery. The lake at top right, west of Lake City, is labeled Lake Lee Guss, which may be Gwen Lake or Lake Harris. The campus of Florida Agricultural College can be seen behind the lake on the land of J.F. Baya. The courthouse is visible on the present-day site of Olustee Park. The Borum House,

also known as the Central Hotel, was at the present-day location of the old Gateway Theatre Building. T.G. Henderson Fancy Groceries is on the corner of Madison Street and Marion Avenue. The house of John Vinzant, noted on the map as John Vanzant Jr. Clerk Circuit Court, is at the corner of Nassau Street and Hernando Avenue.

In 1901, a site was chosen for a new courthouse closer to Lake DeSoto. Pictured is the sixth and present-day Columbia County Courthouse in 1902 when it was completed. There was a small park behind the building on Lake DeSoto. The previous courthouse was dismantled and moved to the former residence of Lott Johnson. (State Archives of Florida.)

The Columbia County tax collector's office was built in the 1930s by the Works Progress Administration. The building is where Columbia County citizens go for driver license services, hunting and fishing licenses, concealed weapons permits, and other tax-related services. This photograph of the building is from 1948. (State Archives of Florida.)

In 1883, George O. Adicks organized a group of 24 volunteer to fight fires with a hand pump, bucket, and ladder wagon, creating the first fire department in Lake City. In 1908, a horse was added to the wagon. Adicks is on the left, next to the horse. Lake City local Horace Duncan and his son Moses are sitting on the wagon. (State Archives of Florida.)

Lake City firefighters are pictured around 1914 in front of McCrory's; the firehouse was in the back of the building. From left to right are (first row) unidentified, Pete Lopez, Frank Thompson, fire chief George O. Adicks, and Big Jim the horse; (second row) John Gilbert, Chalmers Horn, George O. Adicks Jr., Richard Adicks, and Arthur Fielder. (State Archives of Florida.)

The Horace Duncan house, seen in the 1970s, was previously called the Pink Magnolia. It was built in 1907 and first owned by Horace Duncan. The next owner was Lt. George W. Herlong in the 1950s, leading to the name Duncan-Herlong House. Herlong was part of a hurricane hunter aircraft crew of 10 who perished at sea in 1955. (State Archives of Florida.)

The State Exchange Bank (left) was first located on the corner of Veterans Street and Marion Avenue. The building still stands but looks different today. The buildings to the right of the bank were demolished for a parking lot. On the side of the present-day bank is a mural of the Ichetucknee River. The Borum House, also called Central Hotel, is visible in the distance. (Lake City–Columbia County Historical Museum.)

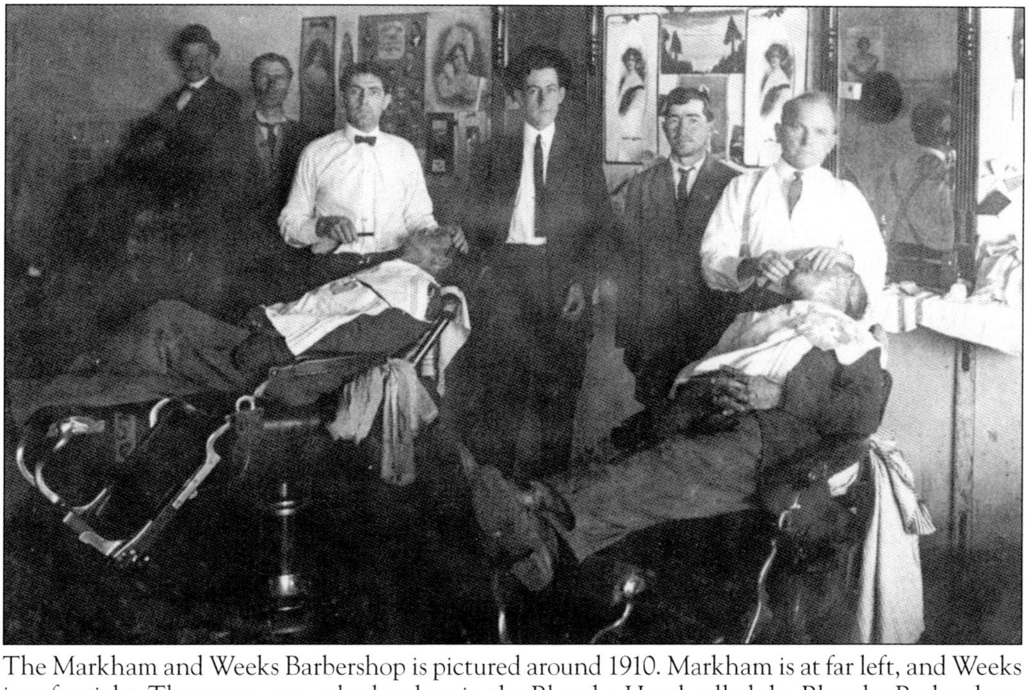

The Markham and Weeks Barbershop is pictured around 1910. Markham is at far left, and Weeks is at far right. There was once a barbershop in the Blanche Hotel called the Blanche Barbershop, but in the 2010s, it moved about one mile south on Main Boulevard during renovations at the hotel. (State Archives of Florida.)

This c. 1910 photograph shows Porter and Glover Dry Goods, run by Porter and his brother-in-law Thomas Glover. The store was first on the corner of Marion Avenue and Hillsboro Street until moving to the corner of Marion Avenue and Hamilton Street. In 1919, Porter and Glover sold their business to McCrorys. (State Archives of Florida.)

The T.G. Henderson House was constructed by George Franklin Barber for Thomas G. Henderson around 1894. Henderson was a wealthy developer and grocer known locally as the "Rockefeller of Lake City." The house was also owned at one time by Dr. Marcello, giving it an alternative name of the Henderson-Marcello House. It was listed in the National Register of Historic Places in 1973. (Author's collection.)

The Blanche Hotel was built in 1902 by Frank Milburn. David William Brown Sr. owned the hotel and named it after his daughter. This photograph of the hotel was probably taken around 1902, when it first opened. In the 1920s, the hotel went through several renovations. In 2017, the building was drastically changed. (State Archives of Florida.)

The interior of the Blanche Hotel is seen here in the 1940s. The hotel hosted many tourists who were either passing through Lake City or visiting the area. Locals say that Al Capone stayed here on his way to South Florida. (Lake City–Columbia County Historical Museum.)

Marion Avenue is the main road of downtown Lake City and is named after American Revolutionary War brigadier general Francis Marion. The Blanche Hotel is seen toward the back, with the balcony on the second floor and the old State Exchange Bank beside it. The building to the left of the

Blanche Hotel also has a balcony but is no longer there. Many of the buildings in the photograph still stand today. This photograph of Marion Avenue is from 1907. At the time, there were only horse-drawn carriages on the road. (State Archives of Florida.)

The State Exchange Bank seen here is the second location of the bank on Northwest Madison Street. In 1983, Barnett Bank acquired the State Exchange Bank and rebranded it as Barnett Bank of Columbia County. In 1990, it merged with Barnett Bank of Suwannee Valley to form Barnett Bank of North Central Florida. In 1998, the bank became NationsBank, and in 1999, it merged with BankAmerica to form Bank of America. The building that was last used by the State Exchange Bank is now Wolfson Children's Specialty Center and Vann Carpet One. (State Archives of Florida.)

Here is the corner of Marion Avenue and Veterans Street in downtown Lake City in 1930. The Blanche Hotel on the left with the large balcony. As of 2020, the road to the right of the hotel is a walking area for shoppers. (H. Morris Williams Collection.)

This is the generating plant on Catawba Avenue in the 1930s. The building next to it was the icehouse. Large blocks of ice were stored there for customers to use at home. The building still stands as of 2019 but has been vacant for many years. (State Archives of Florida.)

This aerial view of Lake City in 1939 shows Lake DeSoto in the center and Lake Isabella at the bottom. The road at center toward the top goes to Waycross, Georgia. The Columbia County Courthouse is at center, to the left of Lake DeSoto. (State Archives of Florida.)

Tourism to Florida increased in the late 19th and early 20th centuries. Lake City's position in North Central Florida along the railroad made the town a popular destination for visitors to stop and rest on their travels. Lake City was also among the top-10 most populous cities in Florida at the time. This public relations photograph for Lake City was taken in the late 19th century. (State Archives of Florida.)

This postcard features a view of city park and the Columbia County Courthouse from the Blanche Hotel in the early 1900s. The public square and surrounding area are drastically different today. A house known as the Chalker residence, partially seen at far left, is where today's parking lot for city hall is located. (Lake City–Columbia County Historical Museum.)

The present-day city hall is the tall building in the center next to a smaller white building. The Blanche Hotel is behind it. The Lake Theatre is on the right. It opened in 1943 and closed in 1964. Today, a parking lot stands where the theater once was. (H. Morris Williams Collection.)

The Lake City Chamber of Commerce was established in 1921 as a voluntary partnership of businesses and professionals in Lake City to better the community. This photograph shows the previous chamber of commerce building on Orange Street in the 1960s. The building has been demolished and is now a parking lot near Olustee Park. (Dr. Christopher M. Esing.)

Marion Avenue is seen in this 1950s photograph. The Blanche Hotel is on the left with several stores in the building. At this time, Marion Avenue was much busier than it is today. Many of the stores seen in the photograph have either relocated or closed. However, a revitalization of downtown Lake City began in the late 2010s. (State Archives of Florida.)

This 1970s photograph shows the Blanche Hotel. Note the partial view of the First National Bank sign at upper right. The Blanche Hotel was no longer a hotel, but there were shops still occupying the space. The balcony had been removed, but its bottom was kept to provide an awning for shoppers. (Lake City–Columbia County Historical Museum.)

The *Lake City Reporter* began with C.A. Finley in 1874 as a country weekly. The paper was not profitable until J.M. Dodd purchased it after moving to Lake City from Kentucky in 1889. He increased the circulation of the *Lake City Reporter* up to his death in 1890. His son Herbert Dodd continued to operate the paper. This photograph shows a crowd waiting for the 1956 election results at the *Lake City Reporter*. Election results at that time were transmitted through newswire and received on teletype machines. (State Archives of Florida.)

In 1959, Lake City celebrated the centennial of its incorporation in 1859. This photograph, taken near the intersection of Marion Avenue and Hamilton Street, shows people celebrating in front of Dubose & Cox in downtown Lake City. Dubose & Cox opened in 1938 and was in business for 22 years until closing in 1960. (Lake City–Columbia County Historical Museum.)

The Columbia Theatre is seen in 1946 on Marion Avenue. In 1967, the theater was renamed the Gateway Theatre. It is no longer a movie theater, but the building still stands. A Regal Cinema movie theater was built a few miles away on US Route 90 and is today the only movie theater in Lake City. As of 2020, the building is owned by Faith Temple Harvest of Life Ministries. (University of Florida.)

This 1970s photograph shows downtown Lake City looking north on Marion Avenue. Over time, businesses on this part of Marion Avenue came and went. At one time, Belk and J.C. Penney were located in this area but later moved to the Lake City Mall. (Lake City–Columbia County Historical Museum.)

Here is the Coca-Cola Bottling Co. building on the corner of Escambia Street and Alachua Avenue. The building is no longer occupied by Coca-Cola but is still standing, with the Coca-Cola logo still on display. Operations at the Coca-Cola Bottling Co. peaked in the 1950s and 1960s. (Lake City–Columbia County Historical Museum.)

Here is the previous city hall of Lake City, in the 1950s. This building was next to the present-day police and fire departments and Popeyes. The entrance to the building, as seen here, was on Main Boulevard. (Dr. Christopher M. Esing, Lake City–Columbia County Historical Museum.)

Seen in the 1980s is the front of the former city hall of Lake City. The building was previously Tyson Auditorium. Concerts, school productions, and community performances were held here. One event was with Gov. Bob Graham and Sen. Claude Pepper campaigning for the reelection of Jimmy Carter. This photograph of the building was taken on Alachua Avenue. The building was demolished, and the space is now a parking lot. (State Archives of Florida.)

Shands Lake Shore Regional Medical Center is on the north end of Lake DeSoto. In 1955, the hospital was established as Lake Shore Hospital District, and in 1963, the Florida legislature created the Lake Shore Hospital Authority. In 2003, the hospital was acquired by UF Shands in Gainesville. The name comes from Sen. William Shands, who advocated for a teaching hospital at the University of Florida in Gainesville. In 2010, Health Management Associates acquired a majority stake in Shands Lake Shore Regional Medical Center until 2018, when Tennessee-based Community Health Systems acquired the hospital. (Author's collection.)

In March 1912, Columbia County Bank was established by John Moreland Sikes and Fred Cone. Cone was the first president, and Sikes was vice president. Columbia County Bank moved out of its building and is now on Hillsboro Street. From 1948 to 2000, the bank was under the guidance of the Green and Summers families. On July 1, 2006, Columbia County Bank was renamed Columbia Bank. It has three locations in Lake City, one in Ocala, and one in Gainesville. The old Columbia County Bank building still stands today next to the old Gateway Theatre. (State Archives of Florida.)

Here is a photograph of Marion Avenue looking south in the 1970s. The buildings at center were demolished, leaving a parking lot by the Blanche Hotel and an empty lot next to what used to be Western Auto. The buildings that were demolished housed the Diana Shop, the Lovely Shop, and McCrory's Department Store. (Dr. Christopher M. Esing, Lake City Chamber of Commerce.)

J.C. Penney and Belk were previously on Marion Avenue in downtown Lake City. This photograph shows Belk, then known as Belk Hudson. Both stores have relocated to the Lake City Mall. (Dr. Christopher M. Esing, Lake City Chamber of Commerce.)

Powers Cadillac sold Cadillac and Oldsmobile automobiles and was owned by Ralph Powers. The building is an example of 1920s Art Deco architecture. In the 2010s, the building underwent major renovations to become the Y.J. Store, an East Asian market. (Dr. Christopher M. Esing.)

The Montgomery Building on Hernando Avenue was constructed in the 1940s as a district office for the Florida Department of Transportation. The building previously housed city hall, the Veterans Service Office, and the American Red Cross. Halpatter Brewing Company, a local brewery, now occupies the Montgomery Building. Halpatter was started in 2013 by Chris Candler, Jeremy Gable, and Jonny Frazier. The name comes from Halpatter Tustenuggee, or "Alligator Warrior," the Seminole chief. Halpatter Brewing has occupied the Montgomery Building since 2017. (Author's collection.)

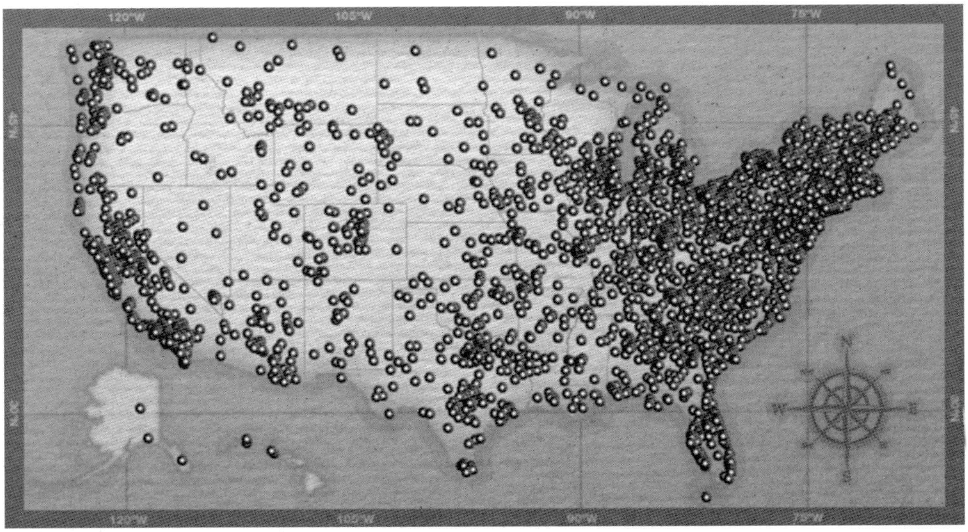